Done is Better than Perfect

7 Keys to Finish Writing Your Book Fast

Author Success Foundations Book 5

by

Christopher di Armani

Copyright © 2018 Christopher di Armani

All rights reserved.

ISBN-13: 978-1988938158

Editor: Nicolas Johnson

Published By:
Botanie Valley Productions Inc.
PO Box 507
Lytton, BC V0K 1Z0
http://BotanieValleyProductions.com

Dedication

This book is dedicated to my sweet and loving wife Lynda. Without her unwavering support none of this would be possible.

Acknowledgments

Without the assistance of my editor, Nicolas Johnson, I can't imagine how this book would read. He tears my words apart from every conceivable angle, then offers thoughtful and constructive criticism on how best to fix the destruction at our feet. I thank God for Nicolas Johnson and his talents, daily.

#EditorsMatter

Feedback Loop

I also wish to express my heartfelt gratitude to the following individuals who took time from their own busy lives to critique this manuscript. Their willingness to assist a total stranger humbles me.

Kim Steadman (KimSteadman.com)
Sharilee Swaity (Facebook.com/Sharilee.Swaity)

Table of Contents

Foreword	1
The Problem	3
Seven Keys to Done	15
1. Self-Honesty	18
2. Clearly Define Your Goals	21
3. Make a Commitment	22
4. Employ Self-Discipline	22
5. Be Consistent	23
6. Be Persistent	24
7. Be Held Accountable	25
The Solution	27
The Road to Success: Become Unstoppable	30
One Last Thing	31
About The Author	32
Books by Christopher di Armani	33
Appendix - Free Writing Resources	39
Endnotes	40

Foreword

Anyone can write a book. Just sit down at your computer and type, right?

We both know it's not so easy. It takes more planning, more determination and more self-discipline than we ever imagined to write a book.

Perfection hides its true nature behind fear, ridicule, procrastination, self-judgment and self-doubt. The search for perfection will destroy your writing life - if you allow it.

Perfection's toxic voice spawns the fear and doubt of procrastination. This demon insists everything is okay - no need to rush. Everything will work out if you would just be patient and stop trying so hard.

This is not good enough. No, this is horrible. You are an unpublishable hack. You can't write. What makes you think you can write a book? This chapter sucks. Just quit already and save yourself the embarrassment.

Lies. Every single one. It will not be okay, not if you fall for the siren calls of perfection and procrastination.

Your book cannot write itself, but that's not news.

In *Done is Better Than Perfect* you learn the Seven Keys to Writing Success:

1. Self-honesty
2. Define clear goals
3. Be committed to achieving your goal
4. Self-discipline
5. Be consistent
6. Be persistent
7. Be accountable

You will learn seven simple steps to transform your book from a stalled work in progress to a completed manuscript.

You will learn how to write more words in less time. You will learn to complete your manuscript in record time and transform yourself from a struggling writer into a published author.

Above all, you will learn the fundamental truths of writing.

Your book will never be perfect.

You cannot publish what you do not complete.

Done is better than perfect.

Learn how to finish your book easier, faster and better than you ever thought possible. Defeat the demons of perfectionism and procrastination.

Your journey down Publication Highway awaits.

Chapter 1
The Problem

Introduction

"Great is the art of beginning, but greater is the art of ending."
— Henry Wadsworth Longfellow

Do you decide, on April 5th, to run the Boston Marathon, then fly to Massachusetts two weeks later? Only if you want to fail.

First, you must design a training schedule to strengthen your body and your mind. You must practice. You must sweat buckets and cry rivers of tears from the pain. Only then, after all the hard work and preparation, do you enter the race and put one foot in front of the other for 26 long miles to cross the finish line.

You write a book the same way.

Set a deadline (your publication date aka the day to run the marathon).

Develop a plan (your training schedule to build your writing skill and stamina).

Implement your plan (train every day) until you cross the finish line (publish your book).

Done Is Better Than Perfect builds upon the habits and systems in the earlier books of the Author Success Foundations series. I recommend you learn the foundation presented in those books first, but *Done* also stands alone, on its own merit.

When you decided to write a book, you decision was only the starting point.

A decision, by itself, accomplishes nothing. Action must follow.

Our sub-conscious mind is a supercomputer with one purpose, to complete every task assigned to it by our conscious mind.

The conscious mind is software. It delivers instructions to the operating system, our sub-conscious mind. The sub-conscious does not care about why - it cares about executing the commands it receives to the best of its ability and without hesitation.

> This automatic, goal-striving machine functions similar to the way electronic servo-mechanisms function, as far as basic principles are concerned. But it is much more marvelous, much more complex, than any computer or guided missile ever conceived by man. It will work automatically and impersonally to achieve goals of success and happiness, or unhappiness and failure, depending on the goals that you set for it. Present it with "success goals," and it functions as a Success Mechanism. Present it with negative goals, and it operates just as impersonally, and just as faithfully, as a Failure Mechanism. Like any other servo-mechanism, it must have a clear-cut goal, objective, or "problem" to work on.[1]

Your mind executes every command you give it with no regard for the "good" or "bad" motives of your desired outcome.

Success, for a writer, comes down to one core principle.

Give your sub-conscious mind correct, specific orders designed to achieve your desired goal.

The purpose of this book is to reprogram your conscious mind with one overriding belief - done is better than perfect.

Your incomplete manuscript holds immense power over you.

It also sustains some of your worst beliefs about writing. Those beliefs must change.

Perfectionism kills.

Done is better than perfect.

If you follow the plan I present in this book, you will reprogram your attitude toward writing. You will write faster and complete your book in less time than you believe possible today.

Best of all, you will learn the simplest and most effective method for writing your next book, regardless of genre or subject matter.

I wrote and published seven books and four workbooks in three months and I did it from a standing start with a single idea - the title of this book.

I practice what I preach. I love writing fast and I love writing well. These concepts are not mutually exclusive, contrary to popular belief. Anyone can write fast and write well. Yes, including you. Let's start with three foundational statements and build from there, shall we?

You cannot edit what you do not write.

You cannot publish what you do not complete.

Done is Better than Perfect.

Every.

Single.

Time.

The Purpose of a First Draft

"Perfectionism is the voice of the oppressor, the enemy of the people. It will keep you cramped and insane your whole life, and it is the main obstacle between you and a shitty first draft. I think perfectionism is based on the obsessive belief that if you run carefully enough, hitting each stepping-stone just right, you won't have to die. The truth is that you will die anyway and that a lot of people who aren't even looking at their feet are going to do a whole lot better than you, and have a lot more fun while they're doing it."

— Anne Lamott

Many writers believe their first drafts must be flawless. We believe the delusion every word flowing from our fingertips must be perfect.

What a pile of self-defeating garbage.

Perfection doesn't exist. Not in the first draft, not in the tenth, not in the one hundredth.

Perfection is a myth perpetrated by our Infernal Editor. Why? Because he cannot comprehend he has no place here. Our Infernal Editor does have a place, but the first draft is not that place.

This brutal truth will, when incorporated into your life, transform your approach to writing.

The purpose of a first draft is to vomit words onto the page.

Nothing more. Nothing less.

Your first draft is a brain-dump of everything you want to say. Toss out those words as fast as you can, every day, until your book is finished. Keep your Infernal Editor on the sidelines, where he belongs.

I created a poster and mounted it on the window in front of my desk to remind me of three fundamental principles.

DONE IS BETTER THAN PERFECT.

You cannot edit what you do not write.

You cannot publish what you do not complete.

As Jodi Picoult described it, "You can always edit a bad page. You can't edit a blank page."

This is the hard truth of every writer's life. Until the words are on the page it is impossible for you to examine the garbage to pick out the gems worth keeping.

Ernest Hemingway said it best.

"The first draft of anything is shit."

I would modify his quote, but only a little.

"The first draft of anything is crap and the bigger the pile, the better."

The more words you dump on the page, the more fodder you have to play with when it comes time to edit.

Abandon your self-defeating belief. It serves no positive role - not in life, not in writing.

Slaughter Self-Judgment

"Artists don't talk about art. Artists talk about work. If I have anything to say to you writers, it's stop thinking of writing as art. Think of it as work."
— Paddy Chayefsky

The first evil spawn of perfectionism is self-judgment.

The job of a writer is not to judge what you write. The job of a writer is to write.

You don't need to judge your work. Not now, not ever. The world will do that for you, all in good time.

Pour those words onto the page in front of you as fast as you can. The faster you write, the more you live in the moment of your story. The faster you write, the less time your Infernal Editor has to inject his unwanted and unnecessary opinions.

Self-judgment has no place in your first draft.

Self-judgment is the murderer of dreams and destroyer of achievement. Slaughter it mercilessly, at every opportunity, and keep writing.

Slaughter Your Fears

Writers live with myriad fears. Fear of success, fear of failure, fear we're lousy writers, fear we have nothing to say and should quit right now, before we embarrass ourselves in front of the world.

Every one of those statements is pure, unadulterated garbage. Every single one.

Whenever you sink into the quicksand of your fears, ask yourself these questions:

1. Is this goal reasonable and achievable in the time frame I've given it?
2. What is distracting me from achieving this goal?
3. What internal resistance must I overcome?
4. What is preventing me from writing in this moment?

My own war is with my internal resistance. Procrastination keeps me from doing what I need to do, when I need to do it. Getting started is the biggest hurdle I face each morning.

The writing?

Simple. Easy. Fun.

So why the internal fight against doing what I love to do, what I know I am born to do? I call it my writer's brain damage. My wife laughs at me every time I storm out of my office screaming I, once again, have *"The Damage."*

My battle, and one I must win each day, is why I implement systems to support my desire to write. The more systems in place, the less my own resistance and desire to procrastinate can derail my day.

But that's me.

I'm sure you never face any of these conflicts.

Whatever your internal fears and battles, face them head on, slay the bloodsucking demons for the vampires they are, and Just Do It.

Write.

Slaughter Procrastination

"The secret of getting ahead is getting started. The secret of getting started is breaking your complex overwhelming tasks into small manageable tasks, and then starting on the first one."

— Mark Twain

Writing is easy. For me, getting started is the hard part so I resorted to self-deception as a way to deal with my procrastination.

Alcoholics Anonymous teaches it is not the 5th, 10th or 20th drink that gets you drunk, it's the first one. This principle, applied to writing, means the hardest word to write is not the 20th, 10th, or even the 5th - it's the first one.

My daily challenge is to Get To One. If I can just write one word on the page, I'm golden.

I developed a system to lie to myself, to use my brain's faulty wiring against itself and get the job done. I focus on the first ten minutes and forget everything else. At the start of each writing session, I follow these three steps.

1. Turn on my computer.
2. Open Scrivener, my writing program.
3. I write something. I write *anything*.

Some days I begin with the words *I have no idea what to write*. It doesn't matter, so long as I pound those keys until I fill the screen with words and don't stop. The "right" words show up before the end of two minutes, without fail.

In the end, a productive writing session can't happen unless you get started.

Keep it simple. Your job, your only job, is to sit down at your desk, turn on your computer and write.

I force myself to create a supportive environment. It helps me fend off distractions. I shut my office door. The sign on the outside of it says "Novelist At Work. Do Not Disturb."

I turn off my Internet connection. With its time-sucking vortexes of Facebook, Twitter and email, the Internet is a Black Hole of Doom. Research can (and should) be done before I sit down to write.

I turn off my phone. They can always leave a message. My phone, along with its insistent notification messages, can wait for two hours. Honestly.

I listen to calming music. Classical is best. Instrumental piano is great, too. Lately, my preference is Gregorian Chant. It puts my brain into a wonderfully creative and productive space.

I set my timer and lie to myself.

I commit to write for ten minutes, no more. I make this promise knowing once I put my fingers on the keyboard, I will pound on it until my eyes cross and my fingers bleed. Mission accomplished.

This a good lie.

If you struggle, like I do sometimes, try a writing timer and see if it helps you too.

Procrastination World Champion

If there was an Olympic event for procrastination, I'd win the Gold medal. I can fritter a day away without putting a single word on the page easier than any writer in history.

The second-place finisher wouldn't even come close.

Despite my world-class procrastination, my editor views me as one of the most productive and prolific writers he's ever known. I laugh every time he says it. Not because it's untrue from his perspective, but because my own subjective view is so different.

Let me give you an example.

When I wrote my first vampire movie, I built the outline during the day. It took me about four months to complete. No problem.

When it came time to write the script, however, my world fell apart.

For the first 3 or 4 days, I berated myself non-stop, but I could not plant my butt in my chair and write. Even when I did eventually sit down at my desk, I would do anything except write. It was horrible.

By the fourth or fifth day I figured out the problem. You see, I did write those first three or four days, but not until the sun went down. When the sun dipped below the horizon, I pounded those keys like a demon possessed until the birds chirped at 4 a.m. I raged at the rising sun as I rushed to finish the scene before I collapsed from exhaustion.

Once I realized this particular story could only be written at night, everything changed. My revelation, and it was a revelation, released me from the self-abuse I heaped upon myself those first few days. I did whatever I pleased while the sun was up, knowing I would pound my keyboard the moment it set. And I did, every night. I completed the entire 120-page script in 21 days. Nights, to be specific.

My mind is a strange place. I accept that.

I share this story to quell your feelings over process. If you cannot write at one time of day, or during the day at all, as I learned with my vampire story, try writing at another time of day. If you're blocked at 9am, try noon. If noon doesn't work, try 10 p.m.

For me and vampire stories, night writing is the only way. It makes no sense, but I accept it. I don't fight it. I shift my workday to accommodate my idiosyncrasies and get on with the job.

Do whatever it takes to get those words down on paper every single day.

Done is better than perfect, remember?

I Don't Know What to Write

Ideas are everywhere.

I can't fall out of bed without half a dozen zipping through my mind, so when I hear a writer complain they don't know what to write, a switch flips inside my brain. I want to scream. I want to slap them across the face with the hope I can rattle some sense into them.

Now, I understand I cannot run around slapping writers for a whole host of reasons, not the least of which is empathy, yet the cold, hard reality remains.

The six stupidest words a writer can utter are:

"I don't know what to write."

Why stupid?

Because the solution is so darned simple.

Contrary to popular myths promoted by well-meaning authors, famous and not, an outline does not suck the creativity out of your life. It does the opposite. A solid, well-constructed outline removes your most powerful excuse. *I don't know what to write* becomes a flat-out lie you can no longer stomach, not if you are honest with yourself.

The beauty of an outline is it speeds up the process. With no need to figure out what to write next, you are free to pour out your first draft as fast as you want. It's great fun.

Notice I did not say creating an outline was easy. I said it was simple. Big difference. Writing an outline is hard because of all the decisions we must make.

Spend 10 minutes to outline the scene you want to write next. Then write it. If this thought offends you, I suggest you try this exercise anyway. Then tell me the words didn't flow out of you like water over Niagara Falls.

I dare you.

Talent vs. Skill

I don't have any talent.

I'm just lying to myself when I say I can be a writer.

Ever tell yourself these lies? I did. Then I realized one simple fact. God gives every one of us talent.

To some He gives more, to others less, but it's not the talent you start with that counts. It's what you do with the talent God gave you that matters.

Don't believe me?

God gave Michael Jordan a little talent.

Not a lot, but some.

In high school, Michael Jordan was cut from the varsity basketball team. At five feet ten inches, he was too short to dunk a basketball.

Here's the most important fact of Michael Jordan's life and, I submit, of your life as well.

God gave Michael Jordan will, self-discipline and a burning desire to compete. What Jordan lacked in skill, he overcame with drive. Sure, it helped when he grew taller, but there are millions of tall guys who don't make it to pro basketball. And of the few thousand who do, only a handful become superstars.

What separates them from the rest?

Drive.

Self-discipline.

Determination.

Their natural talent was the starting point, nothing more.

Limits only exist in our minds. They are the lies we tell ourselves or worse, lies we believe after someone saddles us with their limitations.

Michael Jordan knew one thing above all else. He worked harder and longer than any other player. He would hone what talent God gave him into the mighty skills he used to dazzle the world. He believed he would become the greatest player in basketball history.

Work harder than any other writer. Work longer than any other writer.

This principle worked for Michael Jordan. It will work for you too.

We all start with some amount of talent and determination. While this is our common starting point, where we finish is up to us. If God instilled in you a desire to write, then He also gave you the skill to write. He instilled in you the same thing he instilled in Michael Jordan - the desire to take the talents God gave you and hone them into mighty skills.

Can you imagine a world where Stephen King stopped writing after his 100th rejection letter and became a cab driver, instead?

God gave Stephen King the same thing He gave Michael Jordan - the desire to win, no matter the cost.

Jordan, at age 15, refused to quit after the coach cut him from his high-school basketball team. Like Jordan, King mounted a bigger spike on the wall, slammed his 101st rejection letter on it and kept writing. He honed the talent God gave him into the mighty skill he used to create so many masterpieces.

Make the decision today, right here, right now, you will never quit, you will never give up no matter how many obstacles block your path.

Roadblocks are not put there to stop you. They're put there to test your determination, so develop the will to succeed.

Construct your life so failure is not an option.

Heed the lessons of Michael Jordan and Stephen King. Refuse to quit.

Do you believe they never suffered through a bad day? Hardly. Both struggled mightily with every new failure. What separated them from their respective colleagues was their refusal to quit, no matter what.

Write every day.

Work from an outline.

Inspiration is for amateurs.

The refusal to quit is the source of all the writing cliches we despise. It's also the one quality we must develop in ourselves. .

Goals Without Deadlines Are Just Dreams

When a writer insists goal setting is not effective, they're telling you they don't want to do the work necessary to achieve their goal. It's an ugly truth, but it is truth, nonetheless.

A dream is something you wish for. A goal is a dream with a deadline attached.

The path to done is simple. It really is. Set a deadline. Set a series of deadlines, if it makes your life easier.

I set specific deadlines.

I write a novel by [INSERT DATE HERE].

I write two chapters before lunch.

I write six chapters by 5 p.m. today.

Get the idea?

The power of setting goals is highlighted in the acronym SMART.

- ❑ Specific.
- ❑ Measurable.
- ❑ Achievable.
- ❑ Realistic.
- ❑ Time-bound.

I add a sixth attribute - Uncomfortable.

The goal must push me out of my comfort zone. If I know I can easily write 1,000 words per hour, I challenge myself to write 1,200. When I achieve my increased word count consistently, I set the goal higher.

The goal must push me out of my comfort zone. If I know I can write 1,000 words per hour, I challenge myself to write 1,200. When I achieve my increased word count, I set the goal higher. When I can write 1,000 words in an hour without breaking a sweat, I shorten the deadline. Instead of one hour, I set a deadline of 50 minutes.

The point is to push the limits of my current belief of what's possible. Anything is possible when the right motivation is applied, using correct practice techniques and old-fashioned self-discipline and hard work.

Always challenge yourself to produce more words in less time. In short order you will discover, as I did, you are capable of so much more than you believe.

If you read any of the earlier books in this series you already know the emphasis I place on building your writing life upon the solid foundations of a morning routine, a personal vision statement, and a daily plan to achieve your vision.

Those three keys all begin with the same foundation - honesty. Through a process of honest self-examination, we gain clarity about what is important in the long term, not the current flight of fancy or latest shiny object to pass before our eyes.

In the next chapter, I delve into the Seven Keys to Success for authors, keys designed to get your book finished as fast as humanly possible.

"Remember that fear always lurks behind perfectionism. Confronting your fears and allowing yourself the right to be human can, paradoxically, make you a far happier and more productive person."

— David M. Burns

Chapter 2

Seven Keys to Done

Introduction

"Writers often torture themselves trying to get the words right. Sometimes you must lower your expectations and just finish it."
— Don Roff

Anyone can write a book.

How long it takes you to write yours depends upon seven key attributes:

- ❏ Self-Honesty
- ❏ Clearly-Defined Goals
- ❏ Commitment
- ❏ Self-Discipline
- ❏ Consistency
- ❏ Persistence
- ❏ Accountability

The good news is these are all learned abilities. Human beings are uniquely equipped to learn new skills and develop our character. It's built into our DNA.

These principles and characteristics are not unique to writing. Apply them to every area of your life.

But first, I must dispel two key myths about writing before we move on.

Understand The Purpose of a First Draft

I discussed first drafts earlier, but many writers balk at this thought the first time they encounter it.

The purpose of a first draft is to dump words onto the page as fast as you can.

Nothing more.

When you accept this fundamental fact and embrace it with your whole heart, your entire writing life changes for the better.

Take your outline and turn it into a story, as fast as possible. It does not matter how good or bad the story is in your first draft. Not one bit.

You cannot edit what you do not write.

The key to your finished book is to write consistently, ideally every day.

Never edit while you're writing your first draft. NEVER. Editing is a time-sucking vortex. It stops you from finishing your manuscript. It has no place in your first draft.

Write the entire time you write. Edit the entire time you edit.

Never confuse the two.

Myth: Fast Writing Equals Bad Writing

"Write freely and as rapidly as possible and throw the whole thing on paper. Never correct or rewrite until the whole thing is down. Rewrite in process is usually found to be an excuse for not going on. It also interferes with flow and rhythm which can only come from a kind of unconscious association with the material."

— John Steinbeck

To write fast does not mean writing poorly. It is possible to write 5,000 quality words every day and complete the first draft of an 80,000 word novel in 16 days.

Exhausted from the experience? Absolutely, but your first draft will be finished.

Fast does not equal bad.

To write fast you must begin with a clear outline, a well-designed plot with real characters. This requires planning - immense planning - if you want to write your first draft fast.

A well-constructed outline removes all your decisions. Force yourself to make all the hard decisions long before you write the first word of your story. Only then are you free to pump out huge daily word counts.

Writing, for me, is a three-step process - outline, write, edit.

Step one is the outline, and this can take weeks, months and sometimes years to finish. During this phase, I research every aspect of my story. I plan every twist and turn of the plot. I develop interesting characters and invest the time necessary to uncover every flaw of their personalities.

The process moves at glacial speeds, crushing my very soul each step of the way. Or so it seems.

The second step, writing, is easy. My first draft is a glorious and freeing exercise. Because I removed all the decisions about what to write from the process, my creativity rushes over the waterfall and drenches the page.

My outline allows me to write with blazing speed. I don't worry about what comes next. It's all there in the outline. Read the outline and write the scene. Repeat until complete. Simple.

It's also good quality writing because my creativity flows, uninterrupted.

The editing phase comes last. This is where the true magic happens. This is where my talent, honed into skill through years of practice, comes out to play. The process of refining the raw energy and power of a first draft into a polished story is… magnificent.

I make it sound so simple, don't I? Romantic, even. It is simple and maybe eve more than a little romantic.

Simple does not mean easy. It takes work. Lots and lots of hard work. That's why I don't enjoy the outline phase. It's difficult and I am, at heart, lazy. I want writing to be simple and effortless. All those choices, all those decisions - they wear me out.

Through years of experimentation in the hope I could find an easier road, I grudgingly conceded the fact a well-designed plot in a detailed outline as the easiest way to accomplish my goal.

The pain I endure in the outlining process is rewarded in the latter phases.

I love writing.

I love writing fast even more.

My wife says I glow during the first draft of a project. Her description makes sense, as I feel on fire, like I can't get the words out of my brain fast enough.

I write better, I write faster, and I write easier this way. I also learned I deliver a quality first draft when I write fast from a detailed outline.

If you believe writing fast means writing poor quality content, I ask you to withhold judgment until you work through the process I show you in the pages ahead. If you believe writing from an outline destroys your creativity, withhold your judgment there, too.

Walk with me a little while. Allow me to show you how to write faster and better than you believe possible.

Done is better than perfect, and I will explain how to achieve the first and get as close as possible to the second in record time. All I ask is for you to open your mind and withhold your predetermined objections. I promise you this - you will never write the same way again.

1. Self-Honesty

Author, Know Thy Numbers

"Imagination? It is the one thing beside honesty that a good writer must have. The more he learns from experience the more he can imagine."

— Ernest Hemingway

The key to building an effective writing routine is honesty. How many words do you write per hour and how many hours do you write per day.

If you write 300 words in 15 minutes each day, it's okay. It's enough. When you double your writing time to 30 minutes, you double your output and cut the time to complete your book in half.

Write for ten minutes, without interruption. How many words did you write? Record the number. Repeat the exercise for fifteen minutes. How many words did you write? Record the number.

If your experience matches mine, you'll be shocked.

Quite by accident, I learned I could double my word count by writing for fifteen minutes instead of ten. It sounds ludicrous, yet I found the same results when I increased my writing session from fifteen to twenty-five minutes. I doubled my word count again.

Realistically assess how many hours you devote to writing each day. The number does not matter. Your honesty about the number, however, is crucial. Construct your book on a foundation of truth, not the quicksand of lies. Dishonesty with self leads to failure, never success.

You can improve both numbers. In fact, your word count per hour increases naturally over time and almost without effort. The more consistent you write, the faster you become. The longer and faster you write, the sooner your book is finished.

Here's the key. Both numbers are under your complete control.

When you make the decision to increase the amount of time you write from 15 to 30 minutes each day, you double your output and cut the time it takes to finish your book in half.

Yes, it is this simple.

Author, Know Thy Manuscript Formula

I asked you to honestly assess two numbers - your current word count per hour and how many hours you write per day.

Here comes the fun part, Manuscript Math. I love manuscript math.

$$TWR / WPD = N$$

The variables at play are:

TWR = Total Words Required to Complete your Novel.

WPD = How Many Words You Write Per Day.

N = Number of Days to Complete your Novel.

The average published novel is between 80,000 and 100,000 words. Genres vary, of course, and if you know the specific word count range for your genre, substitute it here.

For this exercise I will use the low end of the range.

TWR = 80,000

How many words you write per day is determined by your word count per hour multiplied by how many hours you write. For example, if you write 500 words per hour and you write two hours per day, your words written per day is 1,000.

WPD = 1,000

Divide your novel's length (TWR=80,000) by your words written per day (WPD=1,000). At this pace, your first draft is finished in 80 days, or about two and a half months.

Increase your daily word count by 50% or another 500 words, and the time required to complete your first draft plummets to 53 days, a week shy of two months. When you increase your word count by another 500 words per day you cut another three weeks of writing time from your novel.

Double your daily writing output to 3,000 words per day and your first draft is complete in less than a month, 27 days, to be exact.

You control the deciding factor: how many words you write each day.

Do you see why increasing your writing time per day is so important? The more you write per day, the faster you write over time. It's inevitable. It's also a phenomenal return on your time investment.

Does this lesson in manuscript math fill you with the desire to add another 15 minutes to your writing session today?

Author, Thicken Thy Skin

"Let me never fall into the vulgar mistake of dreaming that I am persecuted whenever I am contradicted."

— Ralph Waldo Emerson

If you define your self-image by the quality of your writing, you only set yourself up for disaster.

Criticism is an essential component of your development as a writer. The key is to accept constructive criticism about your writing for what it is, about your writing.

It's not criticism of who you are as a human being.

Unlike food, you are not what you write. Writing is your job, your passion, but it is not who you are.

Constructive criticism helps you develop and hone your skills, but only if you have the ears to hear it. A thick skin helps. Separate yourself and your self-worth from the words you write, This is the best thing you can do for your career and your self-esteem.

We all write crap. It doesn't mean *we* are crap.

2. Clearly Define Your Goals
Author, Define Thy Writing Goals

"You need two things to write a great book: imagination and inclination. Without one, your book will be boring; without the other, your book won't get finished at all."

— Ellie Firestone

Whether you are a "plotter" or a "pantser" or believe, as I do, both labels are ridiculous, one thing is clear. To achieve success you must set precise goals. If you don't know where you're going, how do you know when, or even if, you will arrive? You don't.

When you set clear goals, you can chart your progress and gauge your speed to determine if you will meet your goal by your deadline. As I explained previously, for a goal to be effective it must be:

1. Specific.
2. Measurable.
3. Achievable.
4. Realistic.
5. Time-bound.
6. Uncomfortable.

When we challenge the boundaries of "possible" we achieve the improbable.

If you told me, five years ago, I would write a 106,600 word first draft in 27 days, my response would be hysterical laughter.

Five years ago I did not believe I could accomplish such a feat. Likewise, if you told me you wrote 5,000 words per day and did so without difficulty,

I would hang my head in shame and whimper I'm not worthy under my breath. Today, I accomplish both those goals on a regular basis.

The path to both achievements is the same.

Set a goal, put a time limit on it, and work your butt off to meet the deadline.

If I can do it, anyone can.

3. Make a Commitment

Author, Honor Thy Commitment to Thyself

Merriam-Webster's Dictionary defines commitment as "an agreement or pledge to do something in the future."

Commitment is our willingness to do what we said we would do, in the time we said we would do it.

Make the commitment to finish your manuscript. Then take the actions necessary to honor your commitment.

Integrity is our ability, our willingness to employ self-discipline, to take the actions required as a result of a decision we made, and follow through until the end.

4. Employ Self-Discipline

Author, Exercise Thy Self-Discipline

"It's not what we do once in a while that shapes our lives. It's what we do consistently."
— Anthony Robbins

Self-discipline, or self-control, is your ability to control what you do, when you do it and for how long.

Self-discipline determines your level of success, not in writing, but in your entire life. Self-discipline is a muscle, and like all muscles, you strengthen self-discipline with regular exercise.

We want the easy way out. We want the fast road to publication.

We don't want to do the work. This avoidance mechanism is inherent to our makeup, like our need to breathe.

The ability to see the long game, to delay gratification, separates published authors from those who never complete their manuscripts.

Research into self-discipline coined the term decision fatigue to explain how making a lot of decisions over the course of a few hours exhausts our willpower and self-discipline.

This is why I'm such a staunch advocate of building systems to support my desire to write. When I remove unnecessary choices from other areas of my life, I retain the ability, the self-discipline and the willpower required to write every day.

Self-discipline also requires me to abandon my all excuses for not writing.

We're writers. We know we should write. We know we should write every day. Somehow, it's easier to make excuses for why we don't write, isn't it?

"I had a tough day at work. I'll write tomorrow instead."

"The kids are tiring me out. I'll write later."

"I just don't feel inspired. Maybe later."

You can make progress or you can make excuses. The decision is yours.

What wonderful news. You are in control.

The bad news is this: you must be consistent.

You must write.

5. Be Consistent

Author, Write Consistently

"Abandon the idea that you are ever going to finish. Lose track of the 400 pages and write just one page for each day. It helps. Then when it gets finished you are always surprised."

— John Steinbeck

I stress the value of writing every day, of building the habit of consistent effort to achieve your goal, because I'm lazy. I want the fastest and shortest route to my destination.

Race car drivers know the shortest distance through a corner is a straight line. The same is true for writing. The fastest way to a finished first draft is to write every day.

I scoured the earth in search of an easier way, but I could not find one.

If you don't already write every day, develop the habit first and build upon it. Start small. For the first week, write for 15 minutes. You may write longer if you wish, but 15 minutes is the absolute minimum before you call it quits for the day. When you build an unbroken string of small wins, you benefit from the endorphin rush these successes deliver.

When 15 minutes per day becomes easy, bump your minimum writing session to 20 minutes. Repeat this process until you write for 60 minutes every day for two weeks. (I take Sundays off.)

Rewards help.

I hang a calendar on the wall in front of my writing desk. I place a small gold sticker on the calendar every day I meet my minimum word count. My goal for each month is to see an unbroken string of gold stars on the calendar.

Cheesy?

Absolutely. It's also a powerful way to encourage my daily writing habit.

Plus, the cheesy stickers make me happy.

6. Be Persistent

Author, Exercise Thy Persistence

"The hard part about writing a novel is finishing it."
— Ernest Hemingway

Merriam-Webster's Dictionary defines defines persistent as "continuing without change in function or structure."

Google defines persistence as a "firm or obstinate continuance in a course of action in spite of difficulty or opposition."

Persistence is our ability to maintain the course we decided would achieve our goal as fast as possible.

In short, persistence is self-discipline in action.

Do what you know you should do, when you should do it, even when you don't feel like it. This is the fastest path to your published book.

7. Be Held Accountable

Author, By Accountable for Thine Actions

"The only thing I was fit for was to be a writer, and this notion rested solely on my suspicion that I would never be fit for real work, and that writing didn't require any."
— Russell Baker

When I decided to write this series of books, I set a specific goal. I would complete all seven books within 90 days. I committed to this goal publicly. I told my writer's group what I would accomplish and when. I signed my name to my commitment, printed out the pledge and pinned it to the bulletin board on my office wall, where it's a constant reminder.

Another word for commitment is goal - I set a goal to complete this series in 90 days. When I published my goal to my writer's group, it made me accountable to the group. If I did not achieve the goal I set, they would know. It's easy to let ourselves down. It's much harder to let others down, especially when you respect them.

If you don't belong to a writer's group, find one and join it. Find someone in the group you connect with and ask them to be your accountability partner. Share your goals with them and request their assistance to help you stay motivated.

People love to help others. It's human nature.

Put this natural desire to work for you.

DONE IS BETTER THAN PERFECT

Chapter 3
The Solution

Apply the Seven Keys to Success

Done is better than perfect.

You cannot edit what you do not complete.

You cannot publish what you do not edit.

It's all so simple, isn't it?

Hey. Stop laughing.

It wasn't a joke.

Seriously.

Writing a book is ridiculously easy when you break it down into small, manageable steps and work hard to complete those steps within a realistic, yet challenging, time-frame.

Apply the seven keys to success, self-honesty, consistency, self-discipline, persistence, commitment, accountability and goal setting to your writing, every single day.

When you increase your writing speed and the number of minutes you write per day, you will finish your novel in record time.

One more thing…

Challenge Yourself Daily

"Bad writing precedes good writing. This is an infallible rule, so don't waste time trying to avoid bad writing. That just slows down the process. Anything committed to paper can be changed. The idea is to start, and then go from there."

— Janet Hulstrand

The best way to improve your word count and the quality of your writing is to challenge yourself every day.

Did you write 1,000 words today? Fantastic. Challenge yourself to write 1,100 words tomorrow. Work hard until you meet your increased goal seven days in a row. Then increase it again.

Is your goal well-defined?

Does it contain a specific deadline?

Is your deadline achievable, but a little difficult?

Does it push you out of your comfort zone? If so, excellent. Carry on.

Always challenge yourself to go farther than you believe possible, to write more words in less time. Human beings are built for challenges. Our minds are designed to meet those challenges. We thrive on it.

If perfection has any place in the writing life it is here, in the arena of personal challenge. Push yourself to achieve the "impossible" and tear down your internal barriers to success.

Anyone can write 80,000 words in a month. Most writers don't believe it is possible and, because of their negative self-talk, they fail to accomplish it.

Your mind is the most powerful computer on earth. It believes anything you tell it, without question and without fail. Reprogram your self-talk script. Tell yourself you can write 1,000 words more than you do today. Your mind will find a way to accomplish this near-impossible feat.

In less than 30 days, my word count grew from 2,500 words per day comfortably, to over 5,000. If anything, those 5,000 words per day felt easier to write *because* I believed it was possible.

I expected it from myself.

I was unhappy when my count dipped below 5,000. The benefit of my expectation is reflected in how easy it felt to write 21,000 words in three days during NaNoWriMo 2017 - a perfectly normal accomplishment, not extraordinary in any way.

Challenge your beliefs in every area of your writing life. No belief is unassailable. Nothing is off limits. Dare yourself to find your true edge of what's possible. If your results match mine, you will search for those limits, but you will never find them.

My current goal is to write 8,000 words per day, consistently. I'll get there, too. Why? Because I believe it is possible. If I can achieve that goal once, and I already have, I can achieve it every single day.

So can you.

The more you challenge yourself in every aspect of your writing life, the more improvements you make. Exercise your self-discipline daily. Learn to honor your commitment to yourself just as you would to the person you respect most in the world.

Ask fellow writers to be your accountability partners. Find someone in your writer's group, be it local or online, and ask them to help keep you focused and motivated to finish.

Add specific penalties for failing to meet your goals. Be creative with your punishments. For added incentive, make it something you despise, like giving a donation to a charity whose purpose you oppose.

Reward yourself with a treat, as I do with little gold stars on my calendar each day and sour cream and onion potato chips when I publish a book.

It works.

The Road to Success: Become Unstoppable

The first time my editor called me unstoppable, I laughed out loud. It was the funniest thing I've ever heard. I don't view myself as a particularly effective or prolific writer. He does. He jokes about how, if I had a four-hour layover at the airport, I would sit down and write a book while I waited. I wish!

Nicholas is correct about one thing, however. I work hard to improve my skills and increase my capacity to write first drafts in less time. For eighteen years I worked in the film industry, where fifteen-hour days are normal. I'm no stranger to working long hours or working hard. I enjoy doing both. When it came time to leave the industry and write full time, how I worked didn't change. I still worked hard and for long hours.

My entire life, however, I've studied successful authors to learn how they do what they do. I studied their work ethic, their daily writing habits, and any other tidbit of information I could discover to increase my chances of achieving their success.

This book is the result.

Read the sixth book in the Author Success Foundations series, *Become Unstoppable: 7 Habits of Highly Successful Authors* to learn what actions successful authors took to advance their careers.

Then do what they did and watch your writing life explode.

Available from your favorite online book retailers today.

For more information, visit:

https://ChristopherDiArmani.net/become-unstoppable

One Last Thing!

First, thank you for reading this book!

If you enjoyed this book and found it informative (and even if you did not) I would be grateful if you would post an honest review on Amazon and/or Goodreads. Every review helps this book find more readers, the lifeblood of any author.

https://ChristopherDiArmani.net/review-done-goodreads

https://ChristopherDiArmani.net/review-done-amazon

Your support in the form of an honest review really does make a difference. Reviews help authors sell more books and I read every one as part of my efforts to make my books even better.

I would also be grateful if you shared a link to this book on your social media accounts.

If, for some reason, you did not like this book or didn't get what you expected out of it please tell me directly. I will use your constructive criticism to fix any flaws in my book so it better meets your expectations. Please contact me here:

https://ChristopherDiArmani.net/Contact

Thank you so much for your support, feedback and your honest reviews.

Sincerely,

Christopher di Armani

Author Extraordinare

About Christopher di Armani

"Author Extraordinaire"

Christopher di Armani is an Amazon bestselling author and the creator of Author Success Foundations.

This 7-book series teaches authors at any level how to develop the mindset, daily routines and work habits necessary to unleash their creativity and get their books published.

He has published 16 books and produced 4 documentary films on topics ranging from the craft of writing to civil liberties and politics.

Download your free introduction to the Author Success Foundations series at

https://ChristopherDiArmani.net/AuthorSuccessFoundations

Books by Christopher

Awaken Your Author Mindset: Finish Writing Your Book Fast (Author Success Foundations 1)

https://ChristopherDiArmani.net/author-mindset

https://ChristopherDiArmani.net/author-mindset-workbook

Learn how to develop your bullet-proof Author Mindset and create a system guaranteed to deliver success and to build the habits required to work this system every single day.

The choice is yours. If you continue to do what you've always done you'll just get what you already have, an unfinished manuscript and all the disappointment, discarded dreams and self-loathing you can handle.

You will never finish your book.

Now, imagine the possible...

Allow me to be your guide to help you construct a mindset, a solid foundation to complete your manuscript so published becomes, not just possible, but inevitable. This is the power of the Author Mindset.

Design Your Morning Routine: Jump-Start Your Writing Success (Author Success Foundations Book 2)

https://ChristopherDiArmani.net/morning-routine

https://ChristopherDiArmani.net/morning-routine-workbook

There is no magic to writing a book. None. You take action, every single day, until your book is finished. You plan, schedule and execute the plan. You write.

If you are serious about finishing your manuscript, grab your notebook, a pen, and a cup of your favorite beverage, and join me at the kitchen table. We'll chat about habits, willpower and self-discipline. We'll discuss how the mind functions, what makes a habit stick, and how our willpower fades throughout the day. We'll talk about concrete steps to improve your self-discipline.

Then I'll ask you to complete a series of exercises. These exercises reveal, at a deep level, what's important to you - what you value most in life. This clarity of purpose allows you to create a morning routine designed to jump-start your daily writing output.

Author Focus: Develop Your Author Vision Statement and Laser-Focus Your Writing Career (Author Success Foundations Book 3)

https://ChristopherDiArmani.net/author-focus

https://ChristopherDiArmani.net/author-focus-workbook

Writing is easy. Finishing your book is easy, too.

Focus. Be diligent. Apply self-discipline and determination.

You already possess these qualities. This book would not appeal to you if you didn't.

Your author vision statement is an extraordinary targeting mechanism to guide you to your ultimate destination - the end of Publication Highway.

The exercises ahead serve one purpose - to focus your mind on what you value most - your published book.

Join me and map your personal journey down Publication Highway. Discover what you value most, not just in writing, but in your entire life.

Isn't your ideal future worth the time?

Prolific Author: The Step-by-Step Guide to Write More Words in Less Time and Finish Your Book Fast (Author Success Foundations 4)

https://ChristopherDiArmani.net/prolific-author

https://ChristopherDiArmani.net/prolific-author-workbook

The key to unlock your drive to succeed is knowing why you write. When you understand how your desire to write fulfills your core needs, you transform writing from a chore to be dreaded into the vision you were born to fulfill. Time set aside to write becomes as critical to your life as the food you eat and the water you drink.

If we believe success does not matter, neither does the road we travel to get there.

Success matters. The road you travel to achieve success matters more.

Your daily writing routine is the last piece of the puzzle to build a life focused on accomplishing your goal - a finished and published book.

Done is Better than Perfect: 7 Keys to Finish Writing Your Book Fast (Author Success Foundations 5)

https://ChristopherDiArmani.net/done-better-perfect

Give Up Your Perfectionism and Publish Your Book

The three fundamental truths of writing are:

1. Your book will never be perfect.

2. You cannot publish what you do not complete.

3. Done is better than perfect.

Learn how to finish your book easier, faster and better than you ever thought possible when you apply the Seven Keys of Writing Success.

Become Unstoppable: 7 Habits of Highly Successful Authors (Author Success Foundations Book 6)

https://ChristopherDiArmani.net/become-unstoppable

Success leaves clues.

Figure out what successful authors did to advance their careers, then do what they did. It's the most effective course of action. Simple concept, but we must do the work. You know, the hard part.

In the pages ahead I discuss how each habit works, as well as the lies we tell ourselves to rationalize our lack of forward progress. Finally, I shine the light of truth on the lies we tell ourselves and watch as they scurry away like little cockroaches.

Apply these principles to your life and you'll achieve their success. It's inevitable. All it takes is a pinch of perseverance, a dash of focus, and two cups of hard work.

I Don't Have Time To Write And Other Lies Writers Tell Themselves (Author Success Foundations Book 7)

https://ChristopherDiArmani.net/no-time-to-write

Stop Lying To Yourself.

In this installment of the Author Success Foundations series, I dissect seven lies writers tell ourselves and shine the light of truth upon each one.

Every falsehood obscures a truth we refuse to confront. The job of a writer, any writer, is to face our fears head on, protected by the body armor of honesty and integrity. Only then does the brilliance we etch on the page shine bright for the world to see.

Each delusion corrodes holes in our armor, holes the insidious demons of worry, self-doubt, procrastination and perfectionism slip through to poison us.

The Author Success Foundations series provides the tools and materials to patch those holes, to reinforce and strengthen our armor. The day of battle is here, and we must march ever forward. If we stop, even for a moment, our words shrink under the oppressive heat of our fears and we fail.

Step inside. Face your fears. Show these pathetic demons you cannot be cowed. Own your internal dialog and reshape it into a powerful engine, then use that power to drive down Publication Highway.

The Simple 3-Step Secret to Slaughter Writer's Block And Vanquish it Forever

https://ChristopherDiArmani.net/Writers-Block-Book

There is no more perfect Hell than one where I cannot write. You know that terror, too, don't you? That sense your last remaining creative spark abandoned you some time back. It's sickening.

Let me show you how to extricate yourself from that "perfect Hell" permanently.

TOP SECRET - Inspiration, Motivation and Encouragement - 701 Essential Quotes for Writers

https://ChristopherDiArmani.net/Top-Secret-Quotes

This compilation of 701 quotes delivers inspiration, motivation and encouragement on 39 aspects of writing and the writing life.

You will discover quotes to make you laugh and quotes to make you cry. Some are familiar, like old friends. Others you will meet for the first time. All have a common theme: The Writing Life.

When you need it most, you will find words of encouragement here.

Filming Police is Legal - How to Hold Police Accountable While Staying Out of Jail

I write about police issues regularly. I highlight good cops when I can, but I focus on the problems in our police forces with honesty, integrity and abuse. Every time news breaks about police seizing another citizen's camera or cell phone I receive the same question.

Christopher, is it legal to film police?

The unequivocal answer is a court-affirmed YES. It is legal to film police in every state in the United States of America and in every single province and territory of Canada. That YES comes with specific caveats for the audio portion of a recording depending upon your jurisdiction, and it is critical you know those caveats.

The purpose of this book is to educate mere citizens and police forces alike about the legality of the right of citizens to film police, along with an examination of the legal history supporting our legal right to do so.

https://ChristopherDiArmani.net/Filming-Police

Justin Trudeau - 47 Character-Revealing Quotes from Canada's 23rd Prime Minister and What They Mean for You

On October 19, 2015 Canadians elected their 23rd Prime Minister based on good looks, nice hair and a famous name.

They voted for style over substance.

Our 23rd Prime Minister's entire leadership experience consisted of teaching snowboarding lessons and high school drama. His management experience consisted of administering his trust fund and his ego.

Not a single thought was given to what he stood for, what his party stood for, or what he would actually do once elected to the highest office in the land. That bothered me. That bothered me so much I began to research his much-publicized missteps and that in turn revealed a disturbing pattern within Trudeau's numerous faux pas. That pattern is the focus of this book.

https://ChristopherDiArmani.net/Justin-Trudeau-Book-1

From Refugee to Cabinet Minister: Maryam Monsef's Meteoric Rise to Power and her Spectacular Fall From Grace

Maryam Monsef is the ultimate immigrant success story. She could not speak English when she arrived in Canada at age eleven. Two decades later she became Canada's first Muslim Cabinet Minister.

Maryam Monsef's story begins with her mother, a young Afghan widow who fled Afghanistan for Canada with her three young daughters in 1995. That widow spoke English but her three daughters did not. They brought something far more valuable to Canada: the unshakeable belief they could accomplish anything they wanted, so long as they worked hard.

It's no accident her belief in herself led Maryam Monsef to a Cabinet post. She worked hard to learn English and graduated from Trent University, an impossible accomplishment in her native Afghanistan.

Maryam Monsef became the unwitting scapegoat for Trudeau's broken promise on electoral reform, a promise he knew he would break by May 2016. Her birthplace controversy, her attempts to discredit and insult her electoral reform committee, combined with the Prime Minister's betrayal of her trust, sounded the death knell of her political career.

This, then, is the story of one young woman's meteoric rise to political power. It is also the story of that young woman's undoing at the hands of a narcissistic and self-serving celebrity feminist, Justin Trudeau.

https://ChristopherDiArmani.net/Maryam-Monsef-Book

Appendix - Free Writing Resources

Christopher's Pomodoro Writing Timer

https://ChristopherDiArmani.net/free-pomodoro-writing-timer

Writing Software

http://www.hemingwayapp.com/

https://www.grammarly.com/

https://www.libreoffice.org/

http://www.spacejock.com/yWriter6.html

http://stevenluzern.org/product/hypnosis-creative-writing/

Endnotes

1   Maltz M.D., Maxwell. "Psycho-Cybernetics, Updated and Expanded." TarcherPerigee, 2015. Kindle Edition.

www.ingramcontent.com/pod-product-compliance
Lightning Source LLC
Chambersburg PA
CBHW070858050426
42453CB00012B/2266